PROSPECT / REFUGE

Poems

PROSPECT / REFUGE

Poems

Elaine Sexton

The Sheep Meadow Press

Designed and typeset by The Sheep Meadow Press
Distributed by The University Press of New England

Cover Image: Rick Fox, "Magnolia."
Author Photo by Marina Kariakou

Library of Congress Cataloging-in-Publication Data

Sexton, Elaine.
  [Poems. Selections]
  Prospect/Refuge : poems / Elaine Sexton.
     pages ; cm
  ISBN 978-1-937679-53-8 (softcover)
  I. Title.
  PS3619.E98A6 2015
  811'.6--dc23

All inquiries and permission requests should be addressed to
the publisher:

The Sheep Meadow Press
PO Box 84
Rhinebeck, NY 12514

for Nora

CONTENTS

I.

Sometime Muse   3
Only Sky   5
Cantilever Love   7
Cannot   9
Evidence   10
Resident   12
Neighbors   13
Sonnet   14
Barker   15
"Passione"   16
Siren   17
Broken Sonnet   18
Take Another Little Piece   19
Pastoral   20
Key West: In Relief   21
Refuge   22
~~INTENTIONS~~   23
Art/Work   24
"The Clock"   25
Drive   27

II.

About You   33

III.

oh well   36
Subjects Matter   38
I Wish You Were   39
Three-card Monte   41
Laugh Track   43
Suspect   44

The Sound   45
The City   46
Short Back & Sides   47
Let's   50
Lucy Helps Me Remember the 7 Deadly Sins   52
How to Understand Everything   53
The Woman at My Back   54
Stick   55
Knowing   56

IV.

Poetry & Smoke: A Manifesto   59

Notes & Dedications   62

Acknowledgments   63

I.

Sometime Muse

I did not choose you
chose me. And only

occasionally. And only
when I believe

you are soil not fruit.
Today you come

in a perfect container,
shell of a walnut. And

only because sweet
walnuts are local, and

maybe because of
your clean white bin

slung next to a bucket
of trout and basket

of pears, your stiff
circumference

so clearly marked,
you must want to be

opened. You make it
so easy. A slim knife,

and you pop. Why
the thick skin? The tiny

map of your face, so
well defended, dales

of wrinkles, hills, all
wasted on squirrels.

Of all the nuts, I find
you, so hard, so easy.

Only Sky

You walk not rush into these
pictures, the way you step into air
leaving the house,
leaving the door still open.

What you see is all sky
with a skid of land, a tree-
line, or the dark eddy
of sea lapping over

the foreground, or just
pulling back. If you asked,
I'd say all that oxygen
answers every quarrel

we have with ourselves, each
dissolves in the face
of space, the way a stain
in the sky

makes us want to
stop the car, stop *thinking*,
call a friend to
come out of her house,

her kitchen, leave the burners on,
but come *now*
because beauty is likely to burn up
the minute you turn your back.

You know *life is long*
a friend once offered.
A perfect lie. And who
doesn't think of a flame

when something
embezzles
your breath,
beating

like the memory of taste
or echo of a color
on air.
Only this time

the sky is my witness
as it is most of the time
which is to say
all the time I am alone.

Cantilever Love

This plank, walk, observation
deck of the great Minneapolis
high-rise theatre
reaches out
to the Mississippi
and Saint Paul,

Pillsbury's smokestacks,
so close they are
almost touchable,
the mother/structure,
left behind, sturdy,

weight-bearing,
safe. I stand, suspended,
midair, on metal/cement,
cantilevered. So much depends
on what we can't touch.

I reach my face
over the edge, past
glass barriers. Spray
from the great river reaches back.
We almost touch. Tender.

Architectural.
I've come here in splints,
jerry-rigged,
insupportable.
It's touching the way

the body keeps
trying, the body
built to house the brain,
the brain built to house the senses,
the senses themselves

containment facilities,
at once restless and
content to flare up,
die out. Some,
in cantilever moods,

step out. The sun
fixes itself on the skin
which, in turn, contracts
the way the optic
nerve does. In the dark

white jasmine
opens, and exhales.
Hairs in the nose,
tiny cantilevered planks,
reach out to carry

the scent
back to the brain.
My tongue, cantilevered
from my mouth,
touches the fine down

on the nape of your neck
and lifts
not exactly a flavor
but an idea,
suspended, blindfolded, balanced.

Cannot

I can't say *yes* though it presses
my teeth forcing my mouth
open. I can't say why
though each time the village
church bell rings I imagine
what I can't do
being done. I can't see
past the beat
of rain matching my pulse,
this attachment to time
to slow it to employ it.

Evidence

I thought I knew what work was.
I thought I knew what work was
before watching an artist work
at makework in a gallery,
watching a video she made
of herself knocking down a fake
wall in a fake sheet-rocked room
she walled herself in
wearing a red satin dress
and high heels, using a sledge-
hammer to get out, her fake
manual labor making me sweat,
making me mad, making me
self-consciously watch
the museum guard, silent, at his job
watching me watching her
work at her craft. I thought I knew
art work was work at the time,
but just then my dead mother
entered the room
wearing a blue satin dress
she stitched before I was born,
the one she worked
to construct, learning to sew
to please my father.
He sent her to school to learn
how to mend, to keep house, to cook,
her own mother too poor
and beleaguered to teach
much of anything
but honesty. An honest day's work.
And she stood there watching
the guard watching me
watching this artist make art,
all of us working at watching

her knock down a wall
she made for herself.
The only other sound in the room
was my blood knocking arteries
banging their cavities. That was all.
And an occasional cough
from the guard.

Resident

I take steel blue
& titanium white

back to my room.
The prospect of paint

is the refuge
of ideas. The sun loads

the mountain
chestnut

leaves with light,
the other nut

trees stand
in the dark.

Cloudage.
The death of spring

is exposure,
bars of what drops

from the sky,
bands where

the hail falls, then rain,
then night.

Neighbors

When she told me the single
cypress at the rim of a cliff
by her rented flat
meant someone died
or is buried there,
we had just
fetched fresh eggs
from another neighbor,
climbing the slow
incline between her home
and mine. The long light
is back. I stand in the sun
and listen to the unkempt
grass and other small slaps
the wind carries up the pass.
Somewhere someone is mowing.
Tiny finches, aggressively nesting
at eye level, leave and come back.
One rests in the branch
of a stone pine tree, tall and divining.

Sonnet

So sitting, gauging, out loud, just how
warm the surface of this stone
and my own skin can be,
the precise knock of the water
hitting the rocks, of the rocks scraping
their peers or betters, dragging them down,
down to the point where the water heaves
itself up over itself, different each time
a completely different configuration, all
different slabs of seaweed, all different
bits of sand and blue crab, sea debris.
Will there ever be an end to refuse?
Garbage. Good garbage, true.
Spent things. Endless, endless evidence.

Barker

When I talk too much or too loud, when I
boast or imagine I'm higher on the ladder
than I am, a splinter finds lodging
in my foot. And my stomach knots
and knocks. *All show, all talk.*
My stomach speaks perfect English.
Her bark is worse than her bite—
this adage comes back from childhood,
along with a discovery, years
later in San Francisco, that a *barker*
is an actual profession. In my home-
town women sold themselves
in *whispers* at the boatyards at night.
At eighteen, decades too late to
join the Beats, I crossed the country
to find poetry in Ferlinghetti's
City Lights. Across the street
in North Beach, a stranger shouted
selling *Carol Doda, Topless!*
& a side show of women he wanted me
to see. Another block, another barker,
& another & another, sex show signs
with giant breasts lit up in neon.
Pairs of nipples, red bulbs, flashed
on books behind glass, sex-sellers
and booksellers on the sticky
sloping side streets. I was thinking
what hounds men can be,
as harsh and as smooth
as that first stiff drink, shot of whiskey,
after hours, underage, the swivel
of torn leather seats, the whoosh
of something I was certain
to like but didn't. Like growing up.

"Passione"

I pull your fingers through my hair
at the movies as if we were
both blind, your hand under
mine. Outside, on the street, lovers,
both deaf/mute, were really
going at it. I mean they were
screaming the air
with their hands, their torsos,
their hair. One of their manes
snakes around her as if
in the heat of a seizure. Medusa.
The film is Italian. *Neapolitan*
lava in lyrics, subtitles that leave us
spelling out: *love is a wound that*
continues to grow, it will never
let you go. I know this, *I know,*
loosening my grip, letting your
hand drop to your lap gently
in the dark. On film, Caruso, oh!
oh! all the unbeautiful women
of Naples, broken hearted, breaking
the hearts they stomp on. That's
Italian, that's what we're told.
A woman smokes, squatting
on a fire escape, flicking a bit of red ash
over our heads. No longer hot.
I know what a volcano is. I know what it is.

Siren

And she *was* blind. And I was going
to the same natural food store
I heard her say she was going to
when we both stepped off
the cross-town bus. A woman helping her,
before something sour happened
between them, backed away
warning me, shaking her head side-to-side.

I had to help, you see, because
of another woman the other day,
the one I passed and didn't offer
a dollar or even change to. And she
really seemed to need it. And only a block away,
under a summer downpour, I stood
under the lid of a doorwell thinking
I should just go back—I didn't
want to get wet. I regretted it then. And still do.

So when I told this sightless woman,
who seemed a little mean,
I was going her way,
she gripped my arm like death,
like a coffin closing over
my forearm. All circulation stopped
over my past transgressions. And
for a block and a half she told me
she had no living friends, only her cat, and
no family but a brother, incarcerated,
with three years left. And she *said* she wasn't psychotic
only suffering from depression and lonely
like everyone else in New York.

Broken Sonnet

Every time, and just now when someone
mentions they saw you
on Broadway walking a new
hound, fresh blood rushes my carotid
arteries as if the heart hadn't punished
this housing enough. Your name
sears the lining of my stomach,
my brain, stressed syllables beat with
my failures, my successes at botching big love,
over and over the way breathing is inevitable
after a long time holding it back.
In the dream, love is the baby in the bathwater,
the soured, spent suds.
Oh, to get that tossed backwater back.

Take Another Little Piece

Here, she said, over the cluttered
dinner table. Everyone was busy
drizzling lemon over the grilled carcass
of the fish one of them caught
that afternoon in the swift water
under a slowly rotting bridge
the color of lichen and dried
blood. Her slender fingers
held the coarsest tuber,
a sweet potato or yam.
I can never get it right. *Darling*,
she said to someone else,
though she was looking
at me. The mother of all ferries
slid by the screened-in porch,
dragging with it the view every twelve
minutes. But who's counting?

Pastoral

Sleeping, my body's a Mack truck,
my chassis so heavy it's sunk
into the manured hillside, the grass
knitted to my face. Without shame
my frame penetrates the next level
which is clay, then gravel, then the water
table, the y table, and x, and z

down here where Dante imaged hell to be
I lie, undignified with freight,
saturated in a way that would be art if art
could be made of such sordid un-
enlightenment. Out of earth
so disturbed: wake up, I love you.

Key West: In Relief

Beauty is a plank in the middle
of the ocean the scholar

quotes Augustine and I quote her
from my notes scratched

on paper, the page itself
a ferry, a craft. Who said

when you see something beautiful
you must change your life?

I copy this in an act of
reciprocal aliveness, to be

replicated, later,
without the slideshow, micro-

phone, listeners,
without my friend

nudging me in common
appreciation. What a relief

to see a thing
reflected. Tonight

a sea flea stowed in a shell
in my satchel springs out,

crossing the table,
leaping.

Refuge

Labastide-Epsairbarenque

We discover an *un*fortified village
la bastide, in France,
built by serfs
as a way to be free,
in Occitan *espairbarenque*
is to live outside
the walls of protection.
Our prospects are our
best weapons. We make love
with our faces, our words,
our intentions.

INTENTIONS

Art/Work

after Kabir

How do you,
asks the guard,
protect a *Landscape*
where there are no trees
or soil;
where satellites
stationed like stars
watch stones and the sea
reproduce freely;
where rain
is transparent
but solid;
where sounds
replace color,
and nothing agrees to
stay on the walls;
where objects
go after ideas?

Does anyone know
what I'm talking about?

"The Clock"

after Christian Marclay

It is 10:20 then 10:21 a.m. on film,
in the movies, as well as
on our wrists, on an
underwater bomb,
in digital/analog alarm time,
in the tick of a Timex, a Rolex,
a Patek Philippe. An E.R. clock's
second hand sweeps slowly,
silently over 10:30. We sit
in a funeral home,
a bedroom, a kitchen, behind
locked doors, on a cinematic
back porch, in a state room,
jury room, bathroom,
among murderers, traitors, mothers,
surgeons, sirens, and cads,
babies, and amputees. We wade
through dust, dirt,
and seawater,
through the airlessness
of a morgue, watch birds
nip the blonde hair of
a starlet. We are in India.
We trip, we fly over Africa,
Kansas, Paris, Manhattan
and Rome, walk a vacant lot
in Los Angeles, a bridge
over a nameless river,
the central square of a New England
town, and it is only 10:53,
and, then, 10:54, and, now,
10:55 a.m here, in New York,
and everywhere
on the Eastern seaboard, and

everywhere in the movies.
More and more people wait
to spend time
watching time.
They flood the sidewalks,
the street, they clot the gallery
hallway outside this room,
waiting, watching each of us leave
to make space. When I pass
through double glass doors
to daylight on West 21st Street
it is 11 o'clock exactly,
February 18, 2011.
There is time. I feel it. I see it.
I was alive then.
You were still breathing
inside, there
in the dark
where I left you.

Drive

My tiny car's tiny engine
groans and hums
the way my mother hummed

a little ditty when
nervous,
the way I do

mulling over something hard
letting my chest
send a message

to my mouth, my mouth
forming a kind of growl
while all along

staying shut. I enter
the on-ramp to the freeway
heading home

from a family visit,
the pedal to the floor,
I pump my chin

toward the dashboard
thinking I'm helping.
I think I hear

my brother's taunt:
*What is it
with women*

and cars? We are old,
old enough,
to equate mobility

with independence.
Real wheels
take me out of state,

escaping the trap
I thought was
the small town. For this

I left the ocean
I left the trees
I left Eel Pond with seabirds

standing on spring ice,
summer surfboards lined up
on the berm

between the sea grass
and the sea.
I left my family of origin,

my buried Lucky in the back
yard, dog heaven,
now home to a chalet

built by strangers,
the chicken coop,
the barn, gone. When

driving I think of love
as a road trip, the soaring,
the break down, jump

starts, the brand new,
and old reliable.
I'm no mechanic

though I once knew
how to change a fan belt
sheared to a thread.

Here the air is fresh.
The new mutt
who travels with me

leaves her nose prints
on the passenger windows
the way my old dog did,

leaving a spot
just clear enough
to drive through. I imagine

she's smiling, or is it the wind
on her furry face
pulling her lips back?

II.

About You

There are so many of you:
the lover you, the "ex" lover
you— you, the best friend, you,
the neighbor, the analyst,
driver, co-worker,

the hover-mother you,
the alarm ringing,
trouble making,
finger wagging, never-listening-
to-a-word-I-say *you*. All the you(s)

who are stand ins for the many me(s),
as referred to in the Second Person
or Third Person, the you I'll call
the "she" I can't stand, I can't live with,
or without, the group "you,"

the sick, and dearly departed,
the dying and
paralyzingly *alive* you, the one who
disappears when needed,
the you that goes by another name

as in when "you" are a dog,
or a tree, or the sea,
or an implement disguised as a plane
landing, or a pen, or the ink
that leaves clues when it dries;

the Rorschach you: blotted, sobbing,
exposing the all-or-nothing you,
the self-conscious, unconscious
trace of you, the you
when the two of you met, fell in love,

settled for *less* than expected,
got *more* than you bargained for,
the you who cannot spend another day,
another minute, another lifetime
of this *bliss* together,

the you I expected, regretted,
ponderous, careless,
the never-look-back you,
the curious, perseverating,
deal-making, deal-breaking

Pollyanna, sky-is-falling you,
the you who is siren and barker, both
sweet and silent, sometimes
humming a tune no one will ever hear,
or *want* to,

the you so few would *ever* understand
because *that* you, the *real* you,
the original, authentic you
who can only be read in translation,
who is *always* an approximation,

cross-cultural, cross-gendered, *ambi-*
everything, all purpose, visible,
irreplaceable,
admired, abandoned only-to-be
recovered,

the you who appears
in every poem I ever wrote
or ever will write, the one I love,
am devoted to, the you who needs no
introduction—that's you—just you.

III.

oh well

A streak of white
fell like wet paint
and landed on the back
of her head,
her shoulder,
and slid down her back—
something a gull
exhaled and left
before landing
on a piling
where a man in a
two-piece yellow slicker
hosed down a rig
infused with
the stink of dead
or dying porgy
carcasses
crated and lining
the Sound side
of the docks.

Even now
I think of her
two years dead,
paint brush in hand
at the beach
or in bed
with nothing on,
the cross on her
forehead
so deep
no one can touch it.
I miss her
and whisper
it doesn't matter

when I try to
keep her alive
and *oh well,*
when I decide not to.
She looks around
for something
to wipe
the gluey white ash
from the nape
of her neck.
Shit—a halo of excrement.

Subjects Matter

–Lucien Freud (1922-2011)

For me, the paint is the person.

All morning erasures. First,
my father, then mother.

Now, you. Of the past I grasp
one handful, then the next,

turning my face to the side,
my lips, gills, opening and

closing. I am crawling to a raft
that can only be reached

in my sleep. My hands, eyes,
touch your face, arms drawing

your body in strokes, not just
nude but obtrusively naked.

I Wish You Were

Awake. Of course,
I wish it were not
4 a.m.

and the TV
news
helicopter

hovering
over
my building,

scanning
the Hudson,
Lower Manhattan

would
go away.
Never again

will that sound
simply say:
"traffic jam,"

or "man
overboard."
The city

as target,
the city
as

launch pad
now
lies on its back,

eyes up,
never really
going

to bed.
I dreamt
I drifted

for a few hours'
peace.
I didn't think of you

for a few
hours
I didn't lament

a thing.
For a few
hours

the rapid
succession
of rotating regrets

chopping
the sky
stayed still.

The older I get
the more important
sleep is. Sleep

the thing
we think there's always
time for

later.

Three-card Monte

Consider the structures
we bank on:
a cardboard box,

love, that sharp
we shill for
to make ends

meet. A friend
once wrote
how he

broke
a woman's heart,
with regret.

Still gambling,
he asks: *how much
for that?*

Love deals.
My job is to watch
for the cops,

no hooded
four-door sedan
to ferry me

back to
the clapboard
in the suburbs. I live

in her hands,
her ringless
fingers. I trade

in her patch
of pavement,
collect debts

on her bets. I
belt a song
to survive, a tune

a barker once
taught me, shouting
the obvious. Ruin

the shape desire
takes before running
to shame.

You remember shame,
don't you?

Laugh Track

My neighbor laughs, then
I laugh.
I've been swayed
to know second-hand *that*
was funny.
I *get* what he got.
I take what a stranger
took in, and let out,
all this energy—air.
In, out. It tracks.
I hear but don't see (on t.v.)
c a n n e d laughter, an invisible
humming around my head,
an electronic inhale,
this is amusing, *this* is when.

Suspect

We are always warring over what
we can't touch to see. There's the
moon again. Even absent the moon
powers over us the way dreams do.
What would be different if thoughts
were speech? I paint you on the
mowing, knowing you doze each
night on a camp cot looking up.
Here the dogged poppy heads wait
to be cut back, leggy, wooden, dead.
Even in this heat the moon drops a
kind of frost, making every thing
look the way love looks losing light,
the dark as sharp as what's lit—with
no one to watch over it.

The Sound

Ice settles in a glass. Another sunset
over a body of water with no waves,
barely moving like this
conversation. The sun drops
right here, every night, and every night
a hush of disappointment, the host
always hoping for more. And even
the glass house with the priceless view
plays a tune she's heard often before.
The sun sets right here, shifting daily,
precisely. Just so. Some nights
there's a cloud, a thin lip breaking the line.
A fog lingers as it fades.
That's how night falls.
In the distance two stick figures,
strokes of a pen on a spit of land,
fishing. One lights up
a cigarette. A star comes out.
Across the Long Island Sound
Connecticut wonders where we are.
And so do I.

The City

Her nose to the ground, urban dwelling
hasn't stifled her olfactory nerves

one bit though the treats here
are decidedly different:

so many curious dogs,
for instance, and the stains

grizzled men leave in the gleam of
Donna Karan and Godiva

doorwells at night. This morning
at sunrise, a rat as fat as a possum

crossed her path. Every morning
Wall Streeters like farmers

pull up their socks,
suck down coffee, leave their lovers

still sleeping as the day wakes.
More sensations than

she could have imagined,
living a life she would have thought grim

compared to seaside phragmites, pine
trees, and sky. She tells me this

knocking her tail against a streetlamp
licking her lips.

Short Back & Sides

The reason it doesn't hurt
when it's cut is

it's dead, the biologist said,
brushing her dead bangs,

the color of bark,
back from her dead

eyebrows reaching up,
surprised we didn't

know this already. The sushi
came just then,

the wait staff with hair
cut severely,

uniformly straight. The rain
pounced the pavement

aggressively, plashing
back, knocking the plate glass

where we sat sipping sake.
For the first time in months

a smile stretched my lips
till they hurt

and I reached for your
dead grey locks,

curling with impunity
in the humidity

exposing the buds of your
ears. So queer,

the Super Cuts mentality
under discussion.

$20.00. Butch
or femme. *Why spend more*

on something that's dead
you said. *Hair:*

the sexual organ
that shows, someone

read. No wonder we pay.
We love our stylists,

clinging, dependent.
My best friend,

someone said.
How we cried

over a bad color
or cut, evocative locks

severed from their nests.
Our scalps let them go.

Dead anyway, right?
Why should we care?

The temperature rose.
Dead strands,

bleached, and gelled,
blown into place,

hugged one Upper
East Side head

turner, then the next,
gingerly passing by.

Someone shook
an umbrella,

someone shook her head.

Let's

It turns out the old dog,
though she's deaf,

likes old movies
in black & white

and sleeps in the cool
shuttered daylight

in the flat
while her mistress

hits tennis balls back-
to-back in class. I gather

my dread and happiness
in a sack and leave

for work as lovers
on screen sing, "let's

fall in love," eyes locked,
"our hearts are made for it."

I pass a too-tanned
matron on Madison,

a doorman sweating
under his cap, and catch

the #1 LTD on Fifth
downtown to my office.

The groan of the bus
echoes my attitude

about work,
about love,

about age, "while
we're still young,"

I swoon back into
"let's take a chance…."

the textured
sheets, the beautiful

night-long dreams, "little
we know of it,"

visit the recently dead,
the unresolved X, "still

we can try." Love.
"Why be afraid of it?"

Lucy Helps Me Remember the 7 Deadly Sins

Lust is the one everyone remembers,
she says. And considering lust

has become synonymous with desire,
she's probably right. Gluttony, Greed, Sloth,

I add, biblically minded, to the list. *Wrath!*
Envy! someone on the bus hisses and,

scrambling, I press the "Please Stop" sign
over my head, then remember: Pride.

How to Understand Everything

By not looking, how clever!
Why didn't I think of that?
wavering over
the price of cheese
in the market. Everyone
turned to see who was
shouting in the alleyway.
I watched a woman turn her back,
opting for the flicker
of news on their faces.

Someone is always shouting
something in the alleyway,
in the subway, on t.v.,
at the game, playing beach
ball. Someone will always
raise her voice to
such a pitch that
everyone must look,
as though seeing registers

more significance. Sound
makes more sense
than sight. That's why
when someone really wants to
let you know
they say: *I hear you.*

The Woman at My Back

listens to a critic
on a headset
intent on not missing
a word. I stand between

de Kooning's house paint,
slash of green streaking
between "Merritt Parkway"
and "Bolton Landing."

My shoulders ache
under the weight of a thing
no longer here, you
getting smaller and smaller,

like a made-up lover
who doesn't know how to drive,
who keeps making wrong turns,
trusting flawed instincts

to love *this* one,
that one,
me.
"When someone you love leaves

they never come back,"
the public intellectual
wrote, privately
in her journal.

Is it any better where you are now,
the land and sea
indecipherable,
the plains of abstraction clear?

Stick

Tonight everyone said yes to a dirty Martini before dinner and this didn't seem to prolong or distort the conversation we were having about corn. It turns out every single hairy bit, what we shuck, absentmindedly, on the porch, in the yard, at the sink in the tiny galley kitchen, is attached to a kernel from the start. Each strand we watch, shifting in a breeze, on camera, in life, by the side of the road, is anchored to a pip. On the couch, I sit stroking the silky, slender strands of a memory, a heat wave, shucking corn on a rock; or by a house somewhere else, so hot we peeled off our shirts, and stayed, half dressed, shucking, talking, the moon a trail in the dark. Your old deaf dog, our sole witness, nosed in the leaves licking the filaments with great anticipation and disappointment. The life of a dog is full of anticipation and disappointment. So, too, our own. But sometimes between sips, between fields, something. Something.

Knowing

Oh, to travel, to step down
into the sunken lane, to be sunk,
to sink and relish the green
gliss of it. I think of Lucy, who
never passed a lake or a pond,
a sea or a sound
she didn't think to slip into.

After my last dip of the day,
my second swim,
the sun dried the sea to salt
on my skin and I think of her
and imagine I know why she longs to,
at every chance, at every coast—swim.
How the water receives her
unflinching, without judgment.
How her body floats
the way she must have floated in utero—

spineless and mindless at first,
no more than a speck,
the way we'd live if we could
let the phones ring, let the texts go,
be so out of touch,
the small print we can barely read
is barely news at all, a shadow,
a stand in for all that's unsaid,
all that's unfinished, unwritten, unread—
for all that becomes a meadow, a sea, a sound
all fluid, all containment, where the sink,
the pleasure, the knowing and
not knowing, the *you* in all things comes in.

IV.

Poetry & Smoke: A Manifesto

I am for a poetry that makes nothing *happen*.

I'm for a poetry that's too young to date, but too old to overlook.

I'm for a poetry that wants to paint.

I was thinking of those huge paintings by Francis Bacon at the Metropolitan Museum last summer. There must have been about fifty of them. I was thinking of the colors, the wide open space in them, the intensity of their shapes after the stun gun of subject matter. I was looking at myself looking at the canvases, standing in front of them. I was seeing myself, later, in his studio, in the chaos of it. I was thinking of his workspace in relation to his work. Order from disorder. I'm for a poetry that *makes order from disorder.* And sometimes *takes it back.*

There's pleasure in some kinds of confinement, like, say, a correctional facility *of your own design.* But that's *not* what a poem is in my book, not exactly, not a correctional facility. I believe poems come from confinement, quarters you make and inhabit for a while. You have to find a good place to spin like the silk worms in the stalls on the dusty side streets of Shanghai. They spin themselves into an elegant net for display, for the tourists. And the net is all a person can see standing there on the sidewalk, not the worms, which aren't really worms at all, but invisible makers that turn into moths, or become a shell of themselves in a jar on a shelf.

I'm for a poetry that sets out to make something clear, something *visually, sonically, spatially pleasing.* Not opaque. Not obscure. Not *overly* sensual, either. Not cloying the way X's poems are (do I have to name names?) overly rhymed, inside and out, sensual for sensuality's sake, poems that fall all over themselves, that make out with themselves, loving themselves and the sounds they make way too much, so there's no room, no love left for the reader. I'm for the reader. I'm for leaving some room for the reader, a lot of room.

I'm for a poetry that is tart, that barks a little, and maybe, sometimes, *a lot*, a poetry that calls attention to itself... but ... then leaves you alone. You know, the way you feel when the neighbor's dog down the hall has finally stopped barking. And there's suddenly silence. And you never thought of silence that way before, of the word: *silence*. But there you are on the couch, grateful to the damn dog for barking, the dog you were, moments before, dreaming of feeding a bad ham to. But now you *love* that dog, because now you can practically *taste silence* in the wake of his bark, a new taste, one you never tasted before.

And speaking of taste, I'm also for a poetry that still smokes. A poetry that sends signals, words that are signs with their smells still attached, a little ash, a little resin, still sticky, still holding onto their scorched antecedents. I'm for words arranged in a way that makes you think about where they come from, word origins, words that take you back to the beginning of something, even if it isn't their *real* beginnings, the places they *actually* come from, but an original place, one you *imagined* into being. I'm for words that were orphans until you gave them a sentence.

Notes & Dedications

"Art/Work" is for Kaye McDonough, based on the poem, "How do you," by the mystic poet, Kabir (1440-1518)

"Barker" is for Stephanie Craig and Ken Mills

"The Clock" is for John Kramer. The title is taken from Christian Marclay's 24-hour video installation made up of thousands of film clips referring to time, spliced and synced, to be seen and heard in real time, originally screened at the Paula Cooper Gallery/New York.

"Drive" is for John Sexton

"Key West: In Relief" is for Eleanor Sexton and Maureen Baldwin

"Knowing" is for Ellen Neff

The italicized passages in "Passione" are quotes from the 2010 documentary film, by the same name, directed by John Turturro on the musical roots of Naples.

"Resident" is for Julie Baugnet

"Short Back & Sides" is for Gillian Francis and Sarah Salm

"Subjects Matter" is for Bronlyn Jones & Robert Bauer, and contains text by Lucian Freud (1922-2011) as noted by William Grimes in *The New York Times, July 21, 2011.*

"Poetry & Smoke: A Manifesto" is for Curtis Bauer

"Prospect/Refuge" is taken from "prospect-refuge theory," a theoretical approach to landscape aesthetics by geographer Jay Appleton identified in his 1975 book, *The Experience of Landscape (John Wiley & Sons).*

"Only Sky" is for Teddy Laurel

Acknowledgments

Thanks to the editors and publishers of the following journals and anthologies where these poems, sometimes in previous versions or with different titles, originally appeared:

About Place Journal "Knowing"
Barrow Street "Lucy Helps Me Remember the 7 Deadly Sins"
bigcitylit.com "Barker"
Bloom Magazine "Cantilever Love," "Short Back & Sides"
Connotation Press "oh well," "I Wish You Were Here"
The Cossack Review "Art/Work"
Fogged Clarity "Poetry & Smoke: A Manifesto"
Hamilton Stone Review "A Woman at My Back," "The City"
Hunger Mountain "Pastoral"
Ocean State Review "Laugh Track"
Plume "Passione"
Promethean "Three-card Monte," "Subjects Matter"
Sinister Wisdom "Believing," "How to Understand Everything"
Two Rivers Review "The Clock"
Salamander "Only Sky"
Upstreet "Key West: In Relief"

"Poetry & Smoke: A Manifesto" appears in *The Practice of Creative Writing* (Bedford/St. Martins), *The Best of Toadlily Press,* and a featured work on the site, *Lambda Literary.* "Laugh Track" will appear in the anthology *Rabbit Ears: T.V. Poems* (NYQ Press).

With thanks to Stanley Moss and the staff at Sheep Meadow Press.

Thanks to the Ragdale Foundation and Tyrone Guthrie Center for residencies giving me time to write and think.

I'm grateful for the generosity of friends in the making of this collection, for what I've learned from Rebecca Allen, Curtis Bauer, James Brasfield, Theresa Burns, Mary Cappello, Peter Covino, Rachel Eliza Griffiths, David Groff, Scott Hightower, Rick Hilles, Laura

Kaminsky, John Kramer, Teddy Laurel, Daniel McCusker, Kaye McDonough, Martin Mitchell, Roger Mitchell, Nancy Reisman, Sue Scheid, Heather Sellers, Ron Slate, Michelle Valladares, Sarah Van Arsdale, Jean Walton, and Ellen Wiener.

In Memory of my brother, John Sexton (1952-2015)
In Memory of Tom Mohan (1950-2014)

To my students and colleagues at New York University, Sarah Lawrence College, BMCC, City College, and my beloved students in the 2 Horatio workshop.